A to Z
How to Bake Breads for Total Beginners

Lisa Bond

Copyright © 2017 by sbBooks

All rights reserved. No part of this publication may be reproduced, distributed, or transmitted in any form or by any means, including photocopying, recording, or other electronic or mechanical methods, without the prior written permission of the publisher, except in the case of brief quotations embodied in critical reviews and certain other noncommercial uses permitted by copyright law. For permission requests, write to the publisher, addressed "Attention: Permissions Coordinator," at the address below.

Lisa Bond
    lisa@atozlisabond.com

    www.atozlisabond.com

Table of Contents

Copyright © 2017 by sbBooks...2
Introduction...5
The History Of Bread..8
Bread Making Equipment..15
   A big mixing bowl..16
   Spatula, spoon, measuring utensils...17
   Loaf Pans...18
   Wire Rack..19
   Electronic scale...20
   Bench scraper..21
   Proofing basket...22
   Peel..23
   Baking stones...23
   Standing mixer...24
   Bread-maker...24
Ingredients..26
   Yeast..26
   Flour..28
Salt..29
Water..29
   Sweetener..30
   Oil..30
   Optionals...30
Mixing, Kneading and Proofing...32
   Mixing...32
   Kneading...35
   Proofing...38
Bread recipes..41
   Basic Bread...41
      White Bread 1..41
      White Bread 2..42
      White Bread 3..44
      Wholewheat Bread 1..45
      Wholewheat Bread 2..47
      Wholewheat Bread 3..48
   Sourdough & Rye...49

  Rye Bread 1..50
  Artisanal Rye Bread...51
  Sourdough Starter..53
  Sourdough Bread 1..55
Amazing Breads..57
 Bread Rolls...57
 Challah..58
 French Baguette..60
 Italian Loaf..61
Bread Making Tips...63
Conclusion...68

A to Z
How to Bake Breads for Total Beginners

Lisa Bond

Introduction

Bread! We have friends over and want to commune with them; we break bread. The simple act of showing friendship and fellowship. If we are short on money, we need to make some dough. The simple start to the bread making process is synonymous with making our way in the world. If we find something amazing, it is the best thing since sliced bread. Sliced bread must have been pretty amazing. Was there anything good before it? No one will ever know. If we are celebrating, we make a toast (which I do not think has anything to do with bread, but I was running out of bread-related things to say.)

Bread is something we take for granted. It is something which has been part of our culture for thousands of years. It is a part of our daily life. We cannot go anywhere without bumping into a slice of bread. From the humble cheese on toast to the mighty sandwich, to the fantastic grilled cheese sandwich, bread is everywhere. We cannot escape it. We will not escape it.

Now that we have that cleared up let's talk bread. We all know what bread is, there is no need to discuss it any further. The real reason you are here is to learn about how to bake really great bread. Well, I am going to tell you how, and more. We will start with some history before we delve into making great bread. From the dough to the finish, I will tell you everything you need to know about the loaf. From oven baked to bread maker, we will go through the various methods at your disposal. From recipe ideas to what you should do with your stale bread (hint: don't throw it away), we will learn about the versatility of this humble yeasty treat.

There is so much that bread can do and so much that you can do with bread. The ingredients are endless, the recipes are endless; the possibilities are endless. Come on a journey with me as we bake some bread.

The History Of Bread

Bread is essential for life, in fact, it has helped to pave the way for our civilizations. Without bread, we may not be what we are today. The discovery of bread in ancient times led to the formation of villages and towns. If it were not for bread, the people of old would still be nomadic, traveling from place to place in search of food. Bread was easily made, easily stored, and provided nutrition to everyone. With bread, there was no need to travel to find sustenance. Bread gave people more time. More time to learn new skills, instead of hunting and fishing. Bread birthed our nations.

If we look back to ancient Egypt, we will find much evidence of bread making. If you were to travel back in time to the Great Tomb of the North Necropolis, in Gebelein, you would find cone-shaped loaves of bread. You would do well not to eat them; they may be a little tough. These loaves of bread were baked over 4000 years ago, though I did say you had traveled back in time, so if you were in the tomb all those years ago, then perhaps it would be fine to eat them but do not eat them now. The loaves have survived the test of time, but I am sure that the taste has not.

The evidence for the importance of bread in Ancient Egypt is weighty. There are carvings, depicting people sat at tables with great slices of bread laid out between them. There are the remains of structures which would have been bakeries or places to bake bread. There are the remains of tools used for making bread. There are even the remains of bread and bread dough.

You may (or may not) have heard of a sourdough starter. A piece of dough, or liquid dough mix, is kept aside from the baking process. The next day, more ingredients are added to make the dough, keeping aside a small amount again. In this way, the yeast is cultivated over many days, giving rise to bread (see what I did there?) This was common practice in Ancient

Egypt. A piece of dough was kept to be used the next day as a 'starter.'

If Pliny the Elder is to be believed (and why wouldn't he?), the foam from beer was used as a leavening agent. The foam from the top of beer would be skimmed off and added to the dough mix. This yeast from the beer would help the dough to rise and give a lighter and airier bread. Other cultures would use a paste made from grapes, which would ferment and give a similar effect.

We cannot talk about Ancient Egypt without comparing it to Ancient Greece. Did they also have bread? Yes! Yes, they did. The very first bread oven is said to have come from Greece. The bread in Ancient Greece was mainly made from barley, with wheat being used to bake bread for special feasts.

In the 5th century BC, the very first baker shop opened, selling bread to the common people. The spread of Greek bakers happened soon after, with bakers appearing in Rome. The popularity of bread rose, and specialty bread entered the fray. From honey bread to military rations, bread began to branch out.

What *is* the best thing since sliced bread? That is a discussion for another day, but we do know that the marvel would have come after 1912. It was in 1912 that Otto Frederick Rohwedder invented the machine which sliced loaves of bread. This was revolutionary until Otto realized that it was not. Bakers would not use his machine. They were concerned that the bread would go stale once sliced up. It took sixteen long years for Otto to invent the machine which sliced and wrapped the bread. Then the bakers could not get enough. Perhaps sliced and wrapped bread is the best thing since sliced bread?

Once bread became commonplace, afforded by everyone alike, bread was brought into the class war. White bread was the bread of the rich. It was white; it was pure, it was the best bread you could eat. The dark bread, the bread with the whole grain, became the bread of the poor. Who would want something so rugged and rustic? Did they not have the time and money to grind down those ugly grains and throw away the inedible parts? Of course, in the late 20th century, it was found that the wholegrain bread was the more nutritious, with white bread really only being good for a classic grilled cheese sandwich. The classification of bread was reversed, and the rich came forward and admitted to the great mistake they had made, they apologized profusely (or maybe they didn't, I can't quite remember.)

Bread making made another jump forward in the 1960s. Traditional bread making has always been a time-consuming process. In 1961 machines were made which controlled the dough more accurately. They would work the dough, controlling the entire process. The period of fermentation was decreased, meaning that bread could be made quicker, but at the expense of its taste and nutritional value. These machines allow for the use of lower quality grains and produce quickly made loaves of bread.

The bread making process was further quickened by the addition of chemicals (mmm, yummy chemicals.) The chemicals speed up the fermentation time and the mixing time. This has allowed large retailers to produce bread quickly and imitate the making of artisanal bread, without the need for skilled professionals. The introduction of bread makers has allowed the general public to imitate the bread making process at home, without the need for any professional training.

Traditional bread making is still a laborious process. It takes time to skillfully mix the ingredients, knead the dough, allow it to rise, and then bake it. It is no wonder that in the fast-paced world, we have turned to machines and chemicals to speed the process of our bread making (and other productions.) Traditionally baked bread is superior. If you are able to spend a few extra pennies, go out and get some bread from a real bakery. You will not be disappointed.

Bread Making Equipment

Before we start baking bread, we need to stock up on a few things (or get them out of the cupboard). It is worth noting that this is an investment. Homemade bread will not only taste better than store-bought bread, will not only be more nutritious than store-bought bread, but will also save you money. Yeah, you heard me right; it will save you money. The price of ingredients for a great homemade look will cost as little as half, or a third, of the price of a basic store-bought white loaf. Granted, it will take you more time to make the bread than to buy it, but it is worth every second.

You may, in your kitchen, have everything you need to get started with some basic bread. Chances are that you will lack some of the more advanced (and somewhat optional) tools. As with most things, you will get better quality if you pay a little more, but this is also not rocket science. Paying a grandiose amount will not really guarantee you a better loaf. There will come the point where the quality of the tool will not become any more beneficial. My tip would be to buy tools which do the job, are of good value, and will not break easily. If they match your kitchen, then all the better.

So, what tools should you have?

A big mixing bowl

You'll need somewhere to mix your ingredients, and what better place than a large bowl. You will be combining a lot of flour, and that stuff is so light, that when you mix it in a bowl, it can have a tendency to spill out over the edges. The rule here is that you can never go too big (well, you can go too big, but you know what I mean.) The other advantage of having a large bowl is that you will have somewhere for your dough to rest and rise. Nothing fancy needed here, just a big ol' bowl.

Spatula, spoon, measuring utensils

It is a pretty good bet that you will already have a spatula and a big wooden spoon. If not, go out and buy them (or one of them). You will use these for mixing the ingredients together. I prefer using a spatula, so get one of those if you can. Silicon ones are great, but you should try and find one with some thickness so that it can withstand the sticky dough when you are pushing it around the bowl.

The other essential which you may already have, are measuring utensils. Measuring cups are great for the dry ingredients and wet ones. Measuring spoons are great for the smaller amounts of dry ingredients. A measuring jug will make it easier to measure and dose your wet ingredients. Try to get a wide range of cups and spoons so that you have one for every occasion. There is nothing worse than trying to work out how much of a five-eighths cup, seven-elevenths is.

Loaf Pans

We will be talking about some optional tools soon, and this one kind of falls in both categories. You can make bread without a loaf pan, but if you are making a classically shaped loaf, then this is essential. You may already have some; you may not. If you do not then go out and buy two. Yes, two! Most recipes make two loafs of bread, but if they do not, you will want to double the recipe anyway. Most times you make bread, it will not last long. You can also slice one loaf and store it in the freezer for making toast.

The standard size for a loaf pan is nine by five inches. Pay a little more money for your loaf pan and get one that is good quality and has a non-stick coating. You could also buy some silicon ones. If you have one with a non-stick coating, make sure not to use anything metallic on it to clean or scrape. If you take care of your loaf pans then you may never have to buy another one again (and the non-stick coating will remain non-stick.)

Wire Rack

It takes heat to bake your bread. When they are done baking, they will be hot. If a loaf of bread is left in a loaf pan or sat on a surface, the steam from the bread will become trapped. If a lot of the moisture is trapped, it will make your bread soggy, and let's face it, who likes soggy bread? Invest in a couple of wire racks to cool your bread on. You do not want to get this far and let a little water ruin all your hard work.

And that is pretty much it. That is all you need to bake some great bread. Of course there are some optional tools which you can buy to make the process easier, and in my opinion, more fun. So, what else might we need?

Electronic scale

Your measuring cups will give you a pretty accurate measurement, but an electronic scale can be beneficial for two reasons. Firstly, it will give you a more accurate measurement. When you are making basic bread, this will not be an issue, but as you advance into more artisanal bread, a little difference in measurement can make a big difference in the loaf. An electronic scale will take away any problems with measuring.

The second reason for using an electronic scale is for ease of recipe use. If you are searching far and wide for recipes, or if you have been handed down a family recipe from a loved one, it may not be set out with the measurements you are used to. Instead of a cup of flour, you need to use 300 grams. What? Now, I have to go google this and get a conversion. I probably need to convert everything else too. It is telling me that 300 grams are almost a cup. How can I measure this accurately? I give up! Do you see the mess you can get yourself into? Get yourself an electronic scale if you do not want to deal with this.

Bench scraper

A bench scraper is basically a piece of metal with a handle on the top. You can use it to scrape pieces of dough from your workspace, and you can also use it to divide your dough into portions. The blade is sharp enough to cut easily through the dough, but not so sharp that it will cut through skin or countertops.

Proofing basket

Not really essential, but if you are one of those people who need to have every single gadget, then this is the one for you. They are curved wooden baskets which come in a variety of sizes. They are great for making artisanal bread. When you are proofing your bread, letting it rise, a basket will help to keep the shape of the bread. As the bread proofs, it has a tendency to spread out. Gravity will do its thing, and the bread will rise up, but also spread out to the side. With the basket, it will rise up more. You can line the basket to give the bread a smooth finish, or you can leave it unlined so that the basket imprints on the dough, giving a patterned finish.

Peel

Not needed, but it sure is fun to use. A peel is a long paddle, usually metal and flat, with a wooden handle. They are used for moving bread, and pizzas, around in an oven. It is also used for taking the bread out and moving it to a work surface. They are generally used for big, deep ovens, so you will probably not need to use one at home, but it sure is fun to use.

Baking stones

Baking stones are great and can be used for more than just bread. It is a large flat stone which sits on the rack in your oven. A baking stone will take you closer to the baking capability of a proper bread oven, without the expense of one. Not essential, but can definitely improve the quality of your bread.

Standing mixer

Mixing your ingredients is not too taxing, but kneading the dough can be. A standing mixer is not essential. Kneading can be learned, and you will get satisfaction from kneading your own bread. It is almost meditative to knead bread which looking out your kitchen window on a breezy fall day. With this in mind, there are times when a standing mixer is a necessity. Perhaps you do not have the hand strength or dexterity to knead your own dough. Do not let this deter you from making your own bread. A standing mixer can be costly, but the cost will repay itself if you make enough bread. Spend a little dough to make some dough.

Bread-maker

Is a bread maker cheating? Who's to know. All I know is that you can throw in all your ingredients and let the machine do the rest of the work. The main advantages of a bread maker are that there is minimal work for you. It will mix your ingredients, let the dough rise, knead the dough, and then bake the bread for you. You can also set timers on some so that you can have freshly baked bread when you wake (or any other time of the day.) What are the disadvantages? Bread-maker bread will taste good, but not as good as bread which has been kneaded by hand. They also have small paddles to mix the ingredients and knead the dough. You will have to remove these from your bread when baked. Now you have two holes in your loaf. Some inconvenience at the expense of convenience.

And that is about it for bread making equipment. If you have the basics, then you can make a wide variety of bread. If you have everything on this list, then you can make pretty much any bread you can imagine.

Ingredients

Bread needs ingredients. That is a fact. You may have all the fancy equipment we listed above, but without ingredients, well, you have an empty bowl. Thankfully the ingredients are relatively simple, and you may already have most of them lying around your kitchen. Let's get started.

Yeast

Yeast is one of the most important ingredients in bread. It is the organism which makes the bead rise. Yeah, you heard me, I said 'organism'. Yeast is a living, breathing organism. It feeds on the sugar in the bread and creates the air bubbles in the bread, making it airy and light. Yeast is readily available in your local grocery store.

There are many types of yeast. The best yeast for starting out is instant yeast. Instant yeast can be added directly to your dry ingredients and activates quicker. This means that your dough rises quicker and it takes less time to create your perfect loaf.

Active dry yeast needs to proof. Before the yeast is added to the dry ingredients, you will need to add it to some warm water (which will also be part of the recipe) and a little sugar. The water should be warm. If it is too hot, it will kill the yeast. If it is too cold, it will not activate. It should be around 110 degrees Fahrenheit Leave it for about ten minutes, and it should foam. If it does not foam, then it is not good anymore.

There is also fresh yeast. Fresh yeast also needs to be proofed before using. Fresh yeast is better than active dry yeast, which is better than instant yeast, though when you are starting out, you will not notice much difference in the taste and texture. Instant yeast will last longer (store it in the fridge) than active dry yeast, which will last longer than fresh yeast. Instant yeast will also make for a faster process from start to finish. What you use is entirely up to you.

Flour

White flour will do just fine when making a loaf of bread. It will give you a nice white loaf of bread. White bread is not the most nutritious bread in the world, but there is something comforting about a large slab of white bread covered in warm butter.

Whole wheat flour will add a little more density to your bread, and a little more flavor Whole wheat flour does change the consistency, so be prepared for that. Using 100% whole wheat flour will make for a more nutritious loaf, but it will become more dense and less fluffy. You could use a mixture of whole wheat and white if you want to get the benefits of both.

Bread flour is a variety of white flour, created specifically for bread. It has a higher protein content, meaning that the gluten works better. Your bread bakes stronger, and you will end up with a more elastic texture. The bread will hold together better and will make slicing it easier.

There are also specialty flours such as rye and oat. You can also use gluten-free flours in certain recipes. If you are using some of these flours, be sure to use them in a recipe that calls for it, rather than substituting them for white or whole wheat. They react differently in recipes, and the recipe will be different to accommodate them.

Salt

There is not much to say about salt here except that it helps the ingredients work together and helps to flavor the bread. Use what the recipe calls for. Your basic table salt is fine.

Water

Pretty straightforward with this one too. You can use purified water if you wish. You can use filtered water. Straight tap water is fine. Make sure to measure it as exact as you can, and if you are using fresh or active dry yeast, make sure that it is at around 110 Fahrenheit, and that the yeast is added to it before adding any dry ingredients.

Sweetener

The yeast needs some sugar to feed on. You can use straight white sugar, or you can substitute another sweetener. Honey works well, as does brown sugar. Most sweeteners can be directly substituted.

Oil

Most recipes will call for some oil. Oils such as canola or olive oil work well. You can substitute butter. Margarine can be used, but I would not recommend it.

Optionals

Whole wheat is better than white flour, but whole grain is even better. Experiment with adding some grains. Oats, seeds, whole grains all work as a substitute for flour. I like to take 2/3 of the flour amount and top it up with a whole grain. This makes your bread super nutritious.

When you have mastered a few basic recipes, think about what you could add and add it. It may be a colossal failure, or it may be the best bread you have ever tasted.

Mixing, Kneading and Proofing

The three main parts to making your dough: mixing, kneading and proofing. All have their variations, and all can affect the outcome of your bread. Let's take a look at each in turn.

Mixing

The first step in bread making is to mix your ingredients. Think this is easy, well think again, and then think again, because it *is* pretty straightforward. You have found your ingredients and measured them out. Now it is time to combine them together.

Take your bowl and dump in the water. If you are using yeast which needs to proof, then add that next and leave it for ten minutes to make sure that it has not died. If it starts to foam, then you are good to go. Add the flour next. By adding the flour after the water, you ensure that none of the flour clumps and sticks to the bottom of your bowl. You will get a nice even mix by adding the water first. Incorporate the flour and water by stirring it around the bowl with a spatula. Scrape the flour form the sides at first, incorporating a little at a time. Make sure to constantly scrape the sides and bottom so that none of the flour gets stuck. Once the flour and water are combining, you can get your nice, clean hand in there too. Fold the dough over itself with the spatula and then push it down with your hand. Squish the mix to make sure that it is thoroughly mixed together.

At this point in time, you have a 'shaggy mess.' The mixture should be formless. It will not be shapely and look like bread dough, yet. It will look a little wet and will be sticky to the touch. If you have the time, you can let the flour and water rest for half an hour. This resting period is called autolyse, and during this time, the flour will become more hydrated. If you let your mixture rest, it will become looser. If you have not let it rest, do not worry, your bread will still be good.

Next, add in your salt, yeast, and any other ingredients. If you are adding yeast which needs to be proofed, you should take some of the water from the recipe and proof the yeast in it. When you are beginning the recipe, pour the remaining water into the bowl and add the flour. At this stage, you will add the yeast and water mix (the amount of water used to proof the yeast does not need to be much, just enough to mix the yeast into).

The salt will help to strengthen the gluten, and the yeast will, well, you should know by now what the yeast will do. Mix by hand for a few minutes more, until the salt and yeast have been incorporated. You now have your bread dough, and it is time to knead it, but before we do, we need to make sure that we have the container you are going to proof the dough in. If you wanted to, you could turn your dough onto a floured surface and quickly wash your mixing bowl. You may have a second bowl to hand. It does not matter what your container is, as long as you oil it so that the dough does not get stuck when proofing.

Kneading

If you have the time, let the dough rest on the floured surface for five minutes. This will help the flour to absorb the water and become less sticky. If you let it rest earlier, you should not have to. If you do not want to let it rest at all, then that is fine too. The easy work is done, now comes the manual labour.

Push the dough downwards and out with your hands. Stretch it flat using the bottoms of your palms. As we stretch the dough, we are lengthening the strands of gluten in the dough. By creating interlocking strands of gluten, we are able to trap the gasses in the bread during the proofing and baking. This will help the bread to be more airy and rise more.

Fold the dough in half and press it down again, stretching it outwards. If at any point the dough becomes too sticky, sprinkle some more flour on the dough, or on the surface. It should be slightly tacky, but it should not be sticking to the surface and your hands. Keep folding the dough in half and stretching it out with the base of your palms.

There should come a point where the dough becomes less sticky, and you will find that you are not needing to add any more flour to it. This is around half-way in the kneading process. Keep going with the folding and stretching. You should aim to knead the dough for between ten and fifteen minutes. When you are done, the dough should be smooth and silky. How do you know when the dough is done?

1. It should be smooth. When you start out, the dough will be a bit of a mess. It will be un-shapely and sticky. When you are done, it should look completely smooth, and it should be slightly tacky.

2. Pick up the dough with your fingers. If it sags down, then it will need a little more kneading. If the dough ball retains its shape, then the gluten fibers have created a strong bond, and your dough is fine.

3. If you press the dough down with one of your fingers, it should bounce back up again. Do not poke your finger straight into the dough ball. Be firm with your poke, but do not assault it.

4. Take a small piece of the dough and stretch it out in front of you. The dough should stretch out until you can almost see through it. If it stays together and does not break, then you have kneaded enough. If it snaps and does not stretch, then you need to knead some more.

5. The main test, though, is the time. If you have kneaded for fifteen minutes, then your arms are probably becoming sore.

If it is not done by now, then it will most likely never be done. Just stop! Stop it! You have done well and deserve a rest.

Proofing

Proofing is where the fermentation takes place. The dough will develop. The structure will be enhanced. The taste will be bettered. The yeast in our door is activated by the liquid in the recipe. Once it begins to feed, it will release carbon dioxide, but where are these bubbles to go? Surely they will escape from our dough? Remember the gluten fibers we created during the kneading? We have created many overlapping strands. These strands now act like a net, trapping the bubbles inside. When the dough rises, you are actually trapping tiny carbon dioxide bubbles inside the dough. There are also other things produced which will help to enhance the flavor

To proof your dough, you will place it in the lied bowl you prepared earlier. You also need to cover your dough. Plastic wrap would be the best coverage as it will keep the heat in the bowl, but you could also use a large cloth. Your dough should rise fine in your kitchen, but if your house is particularly cold, you could place the bowl inside a container with hot water in it. This will help to create warmth around the dough and help it rise.

Your dough is successfully proofed when it has doubled in size. There are cases where you would not want to allow it to grow to quite that size, such as with heavy whole wheat bread, but generally, a dough which doubles in size is ideal. How do you know if it has doubled in size? Well, take a look at it. It does not need to be exactly double. Just take a look, and if it is roughly double the size, your bread is ready to bake.

You can also press a finger into the dough. Before proofing, you wanted the indentation to bounce back. Now that it is proofed, you want the indentation to stay. Most bread will only need proof once, but there are breads which may require multiple proofs. We will not talk about those here. Once your bread has risen, you should lightly shape it into the desired shape and place it in a loaf pan or other pan. You should try not to overwork the bread or you will lose the trapped carbon dioxide and will not have an airy, fluffy loaf. Once it is in the pan, go ahead and bake it.

Bread recipes

You know the importance of measuring the ingredients accurately. You know about how to mix the ingredients together. You know how to knead your bread and proof it. Now it is time to dive into some recipes and have your house smelling like freshly baked bread. Let's start with the basics.

Basic Bread

White Bread 1

Ingredients: 1 1/2 tsp active dry yeast, 2 1/4 cups warm water, 3 tbsp sugar, 1 tbsp salt, 2 tbsp canola oil, 6 1/2 cups all-purpose flour.

Method: Dissolve the yeast in the warm water and allow the yeast to begin to foam. Add in the sugar, salt, and oil. Mix the ingredients together with a spatula. Add in half the flour and mix thoroughly. Slowly add the remaining flour until you have your dough. Knead the dough on a floured surface for around ten minutes and then let it proof for 1 1/2 hours. Once it has risen, divide the dough in two and place each piece in a loaf pan. Let the dough rise for a second time. This should take around forty minutes. Bake the bread at 375 Fahrenheit for thirty minutes or until the bread begins to take on a golden brown color Remove from the oven and place on a wire rack to cool. Each loaf should give you sixteen thin slices or ten thicker ones.

Tips: Make sure that the yeast is active before you add any of the other ingredients.

White Bread 2

Ingredients: 1 tsp sugar, 1/2 cup warm water, 2 1/4 tsp active dry yeast, 1 cup warm milk, 2 tbsp butter, 2 tbsp sugar, 1 1/2 tsp salt, 1/2 cup warm water, 5 1/2 cups white flour.

Method: Dissolve the tsp of sugar and the yeast in the water. Leave the mixture for ten minute stop allow time for the yeast to react. Once the yeast is foaming, add the milk, butter, sugar, salt, and warm water. Mix thoroughly to combine all the ingredients. Add 2 cups of flour and mix thoroughly. Add 3 more cups of flour and get your hands in there to mix the ingredients. Add more flour if necessary. Knead the dough for around ten minutes, until the dough is smooth and elastic. Let the dough proof for around one hour. Once the dough has doubled, divide the dough in half and shape it. Place each piece in a loaf pan and let it rise again. This should take around fifty minutes. Bake the two loafs at 400 Fahrenheit for twenty-five minutes. If you would like a soft crust on the top, brush it with some melted butter. Let the loaves cool and enjoy.

Tips: Cover your loafs when they are proofing in the pans. You can use a tea towel for this.

White Bread 3

Ingredients: 500g white flour (strong white flour if you can find it), 2 tsp salt, 7g instant yeast, 3 tbsp olive oil, 300ml water.

Method: Mix the dry ingredients in a large bowl; the flour, salt and yeast. With your hands, make a well in the centre of the dry ingredients for the wet ingredients to be added in to. Add the oil and the water to the well. Mix the ingredients together, first with a spatula, and then with your hands. If the mixture is too dry, then add some more water. If it is too wet, then add some more flour. Knead the dough on a floured surface. When the dough is silky smooth, and you have tested to see if it is ready, you can begin to proof it. Allow the dough to proof for one hour, until it has doubled in size. Once the dough has proofed, shape it into a ball and place it on a baking tray, lined with some parchment paper. Let it sit on the tray and proof for another hour. Take a knife and cut a cross in the top of the loaf. You do not need to cut very deep. Bake at 400 Fahrenheit for around twenty-five minutes.

When the bread is ready, it should sound hollow when you tap on the top of it. There will also be a nice cross design on the top of it.

Tips: Make sure to add extra water or flour a little at a time. If you want to make the dough ahead of time, you can place it in the fridge overnight, instead of proofing it for an hour.

Wholewheat Bread 1

Ingredients: 3 cups warm water, 1 1/2 tsp active dry yeast, 1/3 cup honey, 5 cups white flour, 3 tbsp melted butter, 1/3 cup honey, 1 tbsp salt, 3 1/2 cups whole wheat flour, 2 tbsp melted butter.

Method: Mix together the warm water, yeast, and first dose of honey, in a large bowl. Add the white flour and let it sit for thirty minutes. The mixture should foam in this time and look bubbly. Add in the first dose of melted butter, the remaining honey, and salt. Stir the ingredients to combine. Add two cups of the whole wheat flour. Turn the bowl out onto a floured surface. If the mixture is extremely wet, then add some more of the whole wheat flour. Add more whole wheat flour as you knead the dough on the surface. When your dough is silky smooth, transfer it to a bowl to proof. Allow the mixture to double in size. This should take around fifty minutes. Once your mixture has doubled, you will have enough for three loaves. Divide the dough in three and place each piece in a loaf pan. Allow the dough to rise a second time, until the dough is an inch above the loaf pan. Bake at 350 Fahrenheit for around 25 minutes. You can brush on some melted butter if you want a softer crust on the top.

Tips: If you want to make one or two loaves, then cut the recipe by a third or two thirds. If you want to save some of the dough for longer, store it in the fridge overnight, or in the freezer for longer.

Wholewheat Bread 2

Ingredients: 1tsp sugar, 2 cups warm water, 2 1/4 tsp active dry yeast, 1/3 cup molasses, 1 1/12 tsp salt, 2 tbsp shortening, 5 3/4 cups whole wheat flour.

Method: dissolve the sugar and yeast in a half a cup of the warm water. Let the mixture sit for ten minutes, until it begins to foam. Add the remainder of the warm water, along with the molasses, salt, shortening, and two cups of the flour. Mix the ingredients well, until they are all combined. Stir in most of the remaining flour until your dough is pliable, but still a little sticky to the tough. Turn the mixture onto a floured surface and knead the dough until it is smooth. This should take around ten minutes. Let the dough proof for around fifty minutes. Once it has doubled in size, cut the dough in half and place each half in a loaf pan. Let the dough rise for a second time. Another fifty minutes. Bake on the lower rack of the oven for ten minutes at 400 Fahrenheit Then turn the heat down to 350 and bake for twenty-five minutes more. When you remove from the oven, take the bread out of the pans as quickly as you can, and let them cool on a wire rack.

Tips: If you do not like the flavor of molasses, you could substitute for honey instead.

Wholewheat Bread 3

Ingredients: 2 cups whole wheat flour, 1/2 cup white flour, 2 tsp instant yeast, 2 tbsp sugar, 1 tsp salt, 1 cup warm milk, 2 tbsp olive oil, 1 egg.

Method: In a large bowl, mix together the flour (whole wheat and white), yeast, sugar, and salt. Mix them all together. Add the milk, then the oil, and then the egg. Beat them into the mixture with your spatula. As you mix, add more flour to achieve the desired consistency. Turn out the mixture onto a floured surface. Knead for around ten minutes. Cover your dough and let it rest for around ten minutes. Shape the dough so that it will fit in a loaf pan, and let it rise for thirty-five minutes. Bake at 375 Fahrenheit for around thirty minutes. If you want the bread to brown less, you can cover the loaf with some foil at around the half-way mark. Allow the loaf to cool and enjoy.

Tips: You can substitute the sugar for honey in this recipe, but add it with the wet ingredients. If you want to make two loaves, simply double the recipe.

White bread and wholewheat breads are the bread and butter of the bread baking world (I said bread a lot in that one sentence). Now that you have mastered these ones, let's move onto some more interesting breads.

Sourdough & Rye

Rye Bread 1

Ingredients: 2 1/4 tsp active dry yeast, 2 1/2 cups warm water, 2/3 cups molasses, 5 cups bread flour, 2 cups rye flour, 1 tbsp salt, 1/4 cup vegetable oil, 1/4 cup cocoa powder, caraway seeds (optional).

Method: Dissolve the yeast and the molasses in the warm water. Let it sit for ten minutes, until it begins to foam. Add the seeds, salt, oil, cocoa powder, rye flour, and two cups of bread flour. Mix with your spatula. Gradually add the remaining bread flour, until you have your bread dough. You may not need to use it all, or you may need to use some more. Turn out your dough onto a floured surface. Knead the dough for around seven minutes. Allow your dough to proof for around an hour and a half. When the dough has proofed, push out some of the air and divide the dough in half. Shape the dough to fit loaf pans, or shape them into balls to bake on baking sheets. Cover with a cloth and allow the dough to rise for another forty-five minutes. If you are baking the dough in rounds, you can score the top with a knife. Cut through the dough a few times. Bake the dough at 350 Fahrenheit for around forty-five minutes.

Tips: You can sub another oil in this recipe, e.g. canola oil. Remember, if your yeast does not begin to foam, it is not good anymore.

Artisanal Rye Bread

Ingredients: 3/4 cups water, 1 tsp instant yeast, 1 3/4 cups rye flour, 1 3/4 cups bread flour, 2 tbsp molasses, 1 tbsp fennel seeds, 1 tsp anise seeds, 1 tsp caraway seeds, 1 3/4 tsp salt, zest of an orange.

Method: You read artisanal at the top, but I bet you were not expecting so many seeds and orange zest! Start by mixing the dry ingredients together. Combine the yeast, flours, seeds, salt, and orange zest. Add in the water and molasses. Mix together thoroughly and add any more flour or water if needed. Cover the mix and let it rest for fifteen minutes. Stir the mix for another minute or two and then let it rest for a further fifteen minutes. Here comes the fun part: cover the bowl and let it sit for twelve to fourteen hours. Go on a Game of Throne binge, or something like that. Once the dough has proofed, shape the bread. Shape it into a long, oblong type shape (or round, if the world oblong makes you shiver). Cover and allow to rise for a final time. This should take an hour and a half (boy, that is lazy bread). Bake at 475 Fahrenheit until the internal temperature of the bread hits 200. Lots of work in this bread, but the result is fantastic, though I totally understand if you want to skip this one!

Tips: If you cannot find bread flour, white flour will do just fine. Make the dough at night and allow it to proof overnight, then bake it in the morning.

Sourdough Starter

Before you can even think about baking sourdough bread, you need to make a sourdough starter. Sourdough bread is not made with traditional yeast, but with yeast from the air. There are some who say there is science behind this, but I firmly believe that it is magic. You will too when you start making your own.

Wild yeast is everywhere. In the air, on our bodies, in our beards (if you have one). It is there for the taking, and once you have it, it will be yours forever (if you take care of it). Wild yeast will give you a taste that traditional yeast cannot. And it is free! You may have heard stories about sourdough starters passed down from generation to generation. Those stories are true. You can begin your own story today. You can create a sourdough started which you can pass down to the younger generations. Your legacy can live on through bread. So how do you make a starter?

Take 3/4 cup + 2 tbsp of flour (white works fine, but you can use any flour you want) and add 1/2 cup of water. Make sure to be exact with your measurements. Mix them vigorously until you have a thick, sticky dough. Place the mixture in a container and loosely cover it with some plastic wrap, or a kitchen towel. Place it somewhere in your house where the temperature remains consistent. You want the container to sit at room temperature. Let it sit for 24 hours.

When you revisit the mix, you should see some bubbles in the mix. This means that it is working. The yeast is making itself at home. Add in the same amount of flour and water as you did at the start. Let the mixture sit as before, for twenty-four hours. We are now on day three. You should see more bubbles in your mix now. Add in the same amount of flour and water again (this is called 'feeding the starter'). Do not worry if you do not have bubbles yet; some starters are slower than others. Mix in the new ingredients and let sit, as before, for a further twenty-four hours.

Day 4: mix in the same ingredients again. Your starter should have increased in volume, so make sure to use a large container for this. There should be a sour smell to your starter. Let it sit again for twenty-four hours.

Day 5: check your starter. If it has not bubbled, or increased in size, then it may not have worked. Do not worry, start again and hope for better luck.

Beyond day 5: keep your starter in the fridge and feed it weekly. After each feed, leave it out the fridge overnight. If you have too much, discard half and feed it. If you are using lots to make bread, feed it more. Keep feeding it, and you will keep it alive. So what now?

Sourdough Bread 1

Ingredients: 2 cups sourdough starter, 1 tbsp melted butter, 1/2 cup warm milk, 1 tsp salt, 1 tbsp sugar, 3 cups flour.

Method: Make sure to feed your sourdough starter the day before using some for your bread. Let the starter sit out the fridge overnight. Pour the two cups of starter into your bowl. Add the butter, milk, salt, and sugar. Slowly add the flour to the mix, stirring to incorporate it as you add it. Keep adding the flour until you have a smooth, slightly sticky dough. Turn out onto a floured surface. Knead the dough until it is like satin. Shape the dough so that to fits into a loaf pan, or shape it into a round shape and place on a baking sheet. Cover the loaf and let it sit for up to three hours. When the dough has risen between one and two inches, you are ready to bake it. Bake at 375 Fahrenheit for ten minutes and then turn the temperature down to 350. Bake for a further thirty-five minutes, checking it when it nears that time. Remove from the oven and place it on a wire rack to cool. Making a starter takes time, but once you have one, it is easy to maintain, and you can make some great bread.

Tips: Take your sourdough starter out of the fridge for a few hours before using it in the bread.

Getting to grips with sourdough and rye? Well, it is time to kick it up a notch. Try these brads to impress your friends and family.

Amazing Breads

Bread Rolls

Ingredients: 1 1/2 cups warm water, 1 tbsp active dry yeast, 2 tbsp white sugar, 2 tbsp vegetable oil, 1 tsp salt, 4 cups bread flour.

Method: What are rolls, if not mini breads. Combine the water, yeast, and sugar in a large bowl. Let it sit for ten minutes, until it is foaming. Add the oil, salt, and two cups of flour. Stir the ingredients well. Gradually add the remaining flour, stirring as you add, until you have the correct consistency. Turn the mixture out onto a floured surface and knead the dough. After about eight minutes, the dough should be smooth and elastic. Allow the dough to proof for around an hour. When the dough has doubled in volume, turn the dough out onto a floured surface once again and divide it into sixteen. Shape each piece into a ball and place on a baking sheet. The sheet should be greased or covered with parchment paper. Cover your rolls with a damp cloth and allow to rise again, this time for around forty minutes. When they have risen, bake at 400 Fahrenheit for eighteen minutes.

Tips: You can sub white flour for bread flour. Freeze some if you have too many or half the recipe for fewer rolls.

Challah

Ingredients: 2 cups water, 1/2 cup margarine, 7 cups bread flour, 1/4 cup white sugar, 1/4 cup brown sugar, 4 1/2 tsp active dry yeast, 1 tbsp salt, 5 eggs, 1 tbsp poppy seeds.

Method: Mix together the water and margarine in a pan. Warm the mixture until the margarine has melted. The mixture should be warm, but do not let the mixture boil. In a large mixing bowl, combine three cups of the flour, the white sugar, brown sugar, yeast, and salt. Once you have mixed them thoroughly, add the water and margarine. Take four of the eggs, and ass them, one at a time, making sure that each one is mixed before adding the next. Begin to add the remainder of the flour, half a cup at a time, until you have the desired consistency. Turn the dough out onto a floured surface and knead for eight minutes, until it is elastic. Allow the bread to proof for an hour. When the dough has doubled in size, turn onto a floured surface and cut into six pieces. Roll each piece until it is long, like a rope. Take three of the ropes and braid them, like you would brain hair. Do the same with the other three to create a second loaf. Place the two loaves on a baking sheet and allow them to rise again, this time for forty minutes. Beat the remaining egg and brush it over both loaves. Bake at 350 Fahrenheit for forty-five minutes.

Tips: Change the thickness and length of your ropes for a different style of finish to your loaf.

French Baguette

Ingredients: 1 cup water, 2 1/2 cups bread flour, 1 tbsp white sugar, 1 tsp salt, 1 1/2 tsp instant yeast, 1 egg yolk, 1 tbsp water.

Method: Mix the flour, sugar, salt, and yeast together in a bowl. When the ingredients are mixed, add the water. Mix with a spatula and your hands. If the mixture is too sticky, add a little more flour. Turn out onto a floured surface and knead for around ten minutes. Allow the dough to proof for around thirty minutes. When the dough has doubled in size, turn out onto a floured surface and cut the dough in half. Shape each piece into a rectangle, eight inches by twelve inches. Roll up the rectangles tightly, making sure that the length is twelve inches. Push out the air bubbles as you are doing this. Roll the dough gently back and forth and taper the ends. Use a knife to cut diagonals into the top of your dough. Once you have done this with both, cover the dough and allow to rise again, for about thirty minutes. Once it has risen, mix the egg yolk and the tablespoon of water to create a wash. Brush this over the top of the dough. Bake at 375 Fahrenheit for twenty minutes.

Tips: Make sure to roll the dough tight, but try not to overwork it.

Italian Loaf

Ingredients: 3 cups flour, 1 tbsp light brown sugar, 1 1/3 cup warm water, 1 1/2 tsp salt, 1 1/2 tbsp olive oil, 1 1/2 tsp active dry yeast, 1 egg, 1 tbsp water, 2 tbsp cornmeal. (+pizza stone)

Method: mix the water with the yeast and brown sugar. Leave for ten minutes and make sure that it begins to foam. Once it does, add the salt and oil. Mix the ingredients together thoroughly. Add the flour, half a cup at a time. Once you have your dough mixture, turn it onto a floured surface and knead for ten minutes. Allow the dough to proof for forty minutes. Once the dough has risen, cut the dough in two and shape into two oblong shapes. Sprinkle the cornmeal on a surface and place the two pieces of dough onto this surface, with the seam side down. Cover the loaves and allow to rise for a further forty minutes. Ten minutes into the proofing, place the pizza stone in the oven and preheat it to 375 Fahrenheit You want your oven and stone hot before baking this bread, and it will take around thirty minutes for the stone to warm sufficiently. Once the dough has risen, mix the egg and water to form a wash. Brush it over both loaves and make a cut down the centre of each loaf, lengthways. Carefully transfer the loaves onto the pizza stone and bake for around thirty minutes.

Tips: Make sure that you place the loaves on something which can be moved, like a cutting board. This will make it easier to get them to the hot oven.

Bread Making Tips

Now that you are beginning your bread making journey, is there anything else you need to know? Not really, but here are some extra tips which will help to make your bread making a success.

•Make sure to read and follow the instructions. They are there for a reason, and all bread recipes are different. As human beings, we have a tendency to skim over the instructions and get cracking on a recipe. We may have made bread a thousand times and skip over one vital instruction which will totally change out bread. Read the instructions first, ask questions later.

• Start small. There is no point in taking on a recipe if it is one which will fail if you do not knead it correctly for seventy-five minutes in an Andalusian cave. If a bread needs careful technique and precision, leave it until you have mastered the basics. You can also start with a more forgiving bread. A focaccia will come out great almost every time. If you mess up a little, it does not matter. Try that one first, or go for a basic white loaf. Start small, hone your skills, then you can go big or go home.

• Be organized. Check the recipe. Find out what utensils you will need and lay them in front of you. Do you need to set the oven to a certain temperature? Make sure to set it ahead of time, so that your oven is ready when your dough is. Find the ingredients. Measure them all and have them ready to be mixed. Run out of yeast? Good job you checked, now you can run down to the store before you have started to mix your dough. Make sure you are prepared, and everything will be better (good advice for life too.)

• Your dough needs you, and you knead your dough (that was pretty bad, but profound at the same time?) Anyway, make sure to take care of your dough. Once you have started kneading, do not allow for any interruptions. Sure, if the kitchen is on fire, then you should probably get out of there, but if the phone rings, leave it; they will leave a message. Feel your dough as you knead it. Become one with the dough. Make it a pleasurable, meditative experience, not a chore.

• Check the bread when it is in the oven. Yeah, the recipe told you to leave it in there for thirty minutes, but after twenty-five, it looks ready. Well, take it out. Not every oven was born equal. That is the great injustice of our society. If it looks like your bread needs less time, give it less time. If it looks like it needs more time, give it more time. If it is browning on one side and not the other, rotate it. Recipes are good to follow, but if something is obviously not correct, then change it.

• Keep track of what works and what does not. If you have a recipe which is to die for, then record it and make it again and again. If you have a recipe that just does not work, throw it out and never use it again. The goal is to make great bread, so give yourself the best chance at doing that.

• Learn from your mistakes. If you can put your finger on what went wrong, then change it. If the bread is burnt on the bottom, cut the bottom off. If the bread is too stale, then use it for breadcrumbs. If it is too soft or too firm, do not worry about it. You can always find a use for your loaf.

• Have fun with your bread making journey. If you are making great loaves, but you are having a miserable time, then perhaps bread making is not for you. Try to find the fun in the procedure. I know that I have found mine. It is most definitely in the eating of the bread.

Conclusion

Well, there you have it. Most bread is made from the same ingredients. To mix it up, we add some new ingredients, knead it differently, shape it differently, or find new ways of gathering the yeast. If you can make one loaf of bread, then you can pretty much make it all.

There is only one secret to bread making: make it with love and take your time. Wait, that was two. There are only two secrets, along with following the recipe. Three secrets. There are three secrets. And, make sure to weight the ingredients correctly. Okay, maybe there are a few secrets, but they are all in the book, so you know them by now anyway.

There is one secret that I would like to add. Not really a secret, more of a tip. The more bread you bake, the better your bread will get. As you bake more and more, you will see what works for you and your ingredients. Bread making is a science, but it is also an art. If you are able to adapt, then your bread will continue to improve.

I was going to leave you with a nice bread pun, but I am all out. I will say this instead: happy baking!